try on
CAREERS
PAPER DOLLS
COLORING & ACTIVITY BOOK

Welcome to this creative and fun
Try on Careers coloring and activity book!

The features of this book are as follows:
Inside there are 20 different professions outfits:
Astronaut, Musician, Scientist, Artist,
Park Ranger, Doctor, Fortune Teller, Life Guard,
Teacher, Dog Groomer, Stylist, Clown, Mechanic,
Gardener, Chef, Magician, Police Officer,
Lawyer, Fire Fighter, and City Planner.
To use this book, * cut out the dolls you see on
the front and back covers.
The cover is made of thicker paper,
so it will work well for your dolls.
Inside the book you will find many career costumes.
Color the costume you like.
* Cut out the costume including the tabs.
Attach the costumes to the dolls by folding in the tabs.
You can mix and match any costume to any doll!
You can even mix accessories and
dresses from different outfits!
You get two sets of costumes to play with - 40 in all!

Enjoy trying on different careers!

* Please supervise your children
when they use scissors, or help them
cut out the dolls and costumes.

Meet The Dolls*

Dorris Doll

Morris Doll

Iris Doll

*Please use actual size dolls on book cover for cutting.

LOOK INSIDE THE BOOK

20 UNIQUE COSTUMES FOR YOU TO COLOR,
CUT OUT AND DRESS THE DOLLS ON THE COVER

LOOK INSIDE THE BOOK

20 UNIQUE COSTUMES FOR YOU TO COLOR, CUT OUT AND DRESS THE DOLLS ON THE COVER

Stylist

Scientist

Artist

Chef

Police Officer

Park Ranger

Musician

Mechanic

Magician

Life Guard

Lawyer

Gardener

Dog Groomer

Doctor

Clown

Astronaut

Stylist

Scientist

Artist

Teacher

Police Officer

Musician

Magician

Life Guard

Life Guard

Gardener

Fire Fighter

Fire Fighter

Dog Groomer

Dog Groomer

Clown

We hope you have enjoyed this paper doll coloring book!

Feel free to leave a review on Amazon!

THANK YOU!

Made in the USA
Columbia, SC
28 January 2025

52829301R00050